Most Interesting: a compendium of articles first published in my local Parish Magazine

All articles within have been researched with little care or attention and should not be relied upon as statements of fact.

Front Cover - Pylon AE 205, Seabrook Road, Exeter.

For Lucky Sue

Contents

Edward VII &VIII

My relatively recent marriage into Kerswell has fostered a surprising new interest; Post Boxes. Yes I know it sounds as dull as ditch water but indulge me if you will.

It was late one evening whilst walking the dogs that I took a short detour to post a letter. Those familiar with the small wall box in the village will know that it has quite a narrow aperture only suitable for standard letters. On the front are the familiar markings ER. Such can be seen on post boxes across the country. More post boxes have been installed during the long reign of Elizabeth II than during the time of any other Monarch.

What caught my eye however was the mark VII. Our local box was cast during the reign of Edward VII (1901-1910). According to one website about 6% of post boxes carry this mark. My (very) limited research suggests there are over 52,000 post boxes in the UK so we have one of around 3120.

This modest revelation led me to wonder whether any Post Boxes had been erected during the even shorter reign of Edward VIII (1936). My limited research suggests that there were about 270 (281 according to Wikipedia) boxes were cast. The majority were Pillar Boxes and whilst many have been removed there are still at least 57 still in use one of which can be found in Peryam Crescent Exeter, Only one 'Ludlow' Wall Box from this time is known to still be in use.

I have managed to bore most of my friends and relatives with this fascinating information and saw no reason not to let my neighbours off the hook. We are now all taking more notice of this British Icon. They are many and varied and are a part of our nation's history over the last 150 years or more. Only this week my Stepson has sent me a picture of a Victorian Wall Box he spotted in the wall outside his Church in Chipperfield.

April 2012

Pictures: Opposite - Edward VIII Pillar Box, Peryam Crescent, Exeter
Above - Edward VII, Kerswell, East Devon

The Sky at Night

If my note in last month's edition about post boxes wasn't boring enough, and I note that there is a Victorian wall box at Stowford Water, I can now report on another exciting pursuit available in Kerswell. OK this might actually be interesting and I apologise if it is. The absence of light pollution makes for wonderful stargazing.

As Sir Patrick Moore and Professor Brian Cox would no doubt tell you, but they are not here so I will, there have been several planets on show in the last month. Looking up at around 10 pm, Jupiter and Venus have been racing across the western sky. Jupiter's four Galilean moons first witnessed by Galileo in January 1610 have been clearly visible with the home telescope. Jupiter is now sinking below the horizon but Saturn is rising in the East. The clear skies in the last week have allowed me to zoom in on the rings. Sadly as the earth rotates at such an incredible speed it was only possible to hold the view for a minute or so, but what a mars-vellous sight it is. Speaking of Mars, this is also visible to the South, a mere 34 million miles away - so with petrol at £1.42 a litre I am not planning to go anytime soon.

For those with the technology, there is a brilliant 'app', The Night Sky, that allows you to hold your iPad (other tablet computers are available) up to the sky and identify the stars and constellations. It has certainly made it a lot easier to navigate the cosmos.

This is not a pastime for the feint-hearted. Clear nights equal cold nights and standing outside directing the household telescope needs both patience and a warm coat. I have the coat!

May 2012

On Cloud 9

In my quest for more fascinating letterbox facts I came across The Letterbox Study Box Group. Yes it really exists and has around 800 members. No it is not about to get 801 but it does have a website at www.lbsg.org. One of their members was in the news last month as having the ambition of documenting the 115,000 or so postboxes across Britain. Peter Wills of Worcester is a retired postie and has already recorded 2,500 postboxes. We will watch out for him in Kerswell.

Last month I wrote about the night sky. Sadly in recent weeks the cosmos has been obscured by cloud. But which cloud I hear you ask. Ok maybe you didn't ask. In any event I don't know - it was dark and there are many to choose from.

The World Meteorological Organisation has ten classifications of cloud starting at 0 and rising to 9. Cloud 9 is Cumulonimbus and is apparently the highest-climbing cloud and hence the expression 'to be on Cloud 9'. Some editions of the scale started at 1 and promoted Cumulonimbus to Cloud 10. My informant, Edna Clouds (OK it wasn't really), tells me that this has since been rectified and Cloud 9 remains the happiest spot in the sky.

I am sure there are plenty of MET Office people locally that can provide a more informed commentary of cloud formation and other meteorological phenomena. I will not attempt the science relying instead on some very limited reading.

We are all familiar with rainbows but have you ever wondered what those beams of sunlight that fan out across the sky are? These are Crepuscular Rays. Minute particles of gas, dust and water make them visible. Digging deeper there are three recognised varieties of Crepuscular Ray. Those that fan out through cloud as columns converging on the sun are are the Jacob's Ladder variety taking their name from Genesis 28 where Jacob dreams of angels ascending and descending from heaven on a ladder.

Of course none of this is as spectacular as the Aurora named after the Roman goddess of the dawn and more commonly known as the Northern Lights. These streaks of multicoloured lights can be seen in the polar regions and I believe recently in Northern England. As cold as it has been in recent months I doubt we will be seeing them in Kerswell in the near future.

June 2012

Clouds form over Mount Vesuvius.

Pylon Appreciation

Imagine my delight to discover that what is probably England's oldest post box still in service is but a short drive into Dorset. Yes, I was bought a book on old post boxes; so more facts to come - hooray I hear you say! The 150 year old Victorian Pillar Box is situated at Barnes Cross, Holwell, near Sherborne (I am yet to visit!) and has a vertical posting aperture (spot the jargon). I gather there was considerable debate as to whether a horizontal or vertical aperture was best. Go on, look it up on the web!

The Olympics will soon be over, Britain's got Talent 2012 is a distant memory and the Eurovision Song contest has been consigned to history only to be mentioned in pub quizzes until it is dusted down in the country that gave us Saabs and Ikea for our pleasure in 2013. Thankfully the Pylon Appreciation Society offers an alternative pastime.

The word Pylon is derived from the Greek, pulōn, meaning gateway, although I note that there is a medical definition meaning a temporary artificial leg. Well at least according to the free online dictionary!

Last year the Royal Institute of Architects awarded a prize of £5,000 in a competition to come up with an Electricity Pylon design for the future. The winning T shape entry was submitted by a Danish firm of engineers Bystrup. The familiar pyramid Pylon was originally introduced in 1928 as a standard design to service the national grid. Over the years it has been modified becoming slimmer with the aid of high tensile steel and computer design. A potted history of Pylon design and development can be found at www.gorge.org/pylons/structure.shtml.

Apparently there are three common designs of Pylon in the UK; the L2,L6 and L12 and are used according to the voltage they carry. Most are of the suspension type where the insulators hang down. Tension Pylons are used where the lines turn a corner and are distinguishable by the insulators that extend horizontally from the Pylon arms. Each carries a plaque with its own number and details of ownership.

A couple of bits of Pylon trivia - the tallest pylons in the UK are 630ft high and are a pair that span the River Thames at Thurrock, next to the Queen Elizabeth II bridge. The widest span created by a pair of Pylons is across the Severn Estuary. Not planning a visit!

So next time you see a Pylon, look at it with just a little more interest. Is it a thing of current beauty or an electric monster?

July 2012

Sorrento Municipal Manhole Cover - could it be more exciting?
(Sorrento comunale Coperchio di botola - potrebbe essere più eccitante?)

Drainspotting

Sounds like trainspotting but can be done in any street, road or lane. No anorak or notebook required. Just look down but do watch where you are going!

There have been drains and sewers since Roman times. Our streets are laden with silent cables and pipes and above them a myriad of access covers. They vary in size, shape, design and markings. Some are ornately decorated, others disguised.

More recently they have been the target of metal theft. In Lagos some suspect that open manholes could be responsible for some of the city's missing person cases. Their manholes have circular iron covers made at great expense by the Nigerian Railways Corporation. In New York over 370 manhole covers have been stolen so far this year. A proposed new law will make manhole cover theft punishable by a maximum fine of up to $2,500 and 30 days in jail.

What is truly fascinating (really it is!) is the many different designs created. There is a museum in Ferrara, Italy housing what it claims to be the largest collection of manhole covers in the world. It seems that anything can become a hobby and get out of control. According to its website this is a private collection run by Stefano Bottoni without VAT. It does not explain the relevance of the tax.

The question of why manhole covers are normally round was, allegedly, used in recruitment interviews by Microsoft to assess how candidates approached a question with more than one answer. That repository of all of human knowledge - the Internet - offers many answers ranging from 'because manholes are round' to 'they are easier to move as they can be rolled' and 'so that some moron from the civil department of your municipality won't be able to drop them accidentally into the manhole' (you can hear the accent as you say it but it is true that they won't fall in). Will the editor allow us a competition for the most original answer?

Now that I am Postbox Hunting, Stargazing, Cloudwatching, Pylon Spotting and Drainspotting; is it any wonder I have a stiff neck!

August 2012

The truth about Greek Islands

Montgomeryshire against Pylons are currently campaigning against a proposal made in March 2011 for a route of Pylons and new sub –station in mid-Wales. Electrifying news for the Pylon Appreciation Society who remain static in their views. However, not everyone is a lover of the Pylon!

Meanwhile the good citizens of Leek have lost their campaign to keep their roundabout. It seems that a revolution was crushed when a group of protesters were removed by the council from their circular campsite. The roundabout and its floral display is to be replaced by traffic lights as part of a £5million development.

The first roundabout to roll onto Britain's public roads, in circa 1909, is at Letchworth – Sollershot Circus - forming part of the world's first Garden City. My usual limited and uncorroborated research tells me that when first built, traffic could circulate in either direction with the requirement to circulate clockwise being introduced in the 1920s.

There is more to a roundabout than first meets the eye. As fashions have changed so has the design of roundabouts. For a period in the 1960s squareabouts were in vogue. These days, so I am told, the fashion has returned to perfectly circular islands. It just shows that everything does a full circle including the fashion in my wardrobe.

Deflection is critical, influencing the speeds at which vehicles enter and exit the junction. A corner on the approach slows traffic whereas the exit should be more gradual allowing vehicles to accelerate away from the junction.

Roundabouts seem to be a very British phenomenon relying on a certain etiquette. It is therefore a surprise to learn that the junction that is claimed to be the first true roundabout is in New York. Strange, as Americans seem to dislike roundabouts and have comparatively few. Apparently the French have more than us but such are their popularity here that there is a Roundabout Appreciation Society.

According to their website, roundabout Jargon includes:

P.M.T. = Painted Mini Traffic Island
A Crusoe = A very large island
A Chevy = A roundabout with sloping chevron brickwork on the perimeter

And if you were wondering where to go on holiday – a 'Greek Island' is a roundabout with a sculpture or monument.

September 2012

Pedal your way around this Greek Island on the inset re-cycled sculpture.
Pedal-about, Seaton, Devon.

Flash-matic

Has anyone seen the Retired Postie yet on his mission to record the UK's post boxes? I was disappointed to note that 'Edward VII', which is how I now refer to our post box, has not been repainted in gold following the Olympics - or at least not last time I looked.

For me, sitting on the sofa and using the TV remote control is multi-tasking. Add to that breathing and persuading Sue to bring me a cup of coffee, well I will leave you to imagine what strain this puts on my otherwise limited mental abilities.

Happily we now have TV remote controls and for this we must thank Mr Eugene Polley of the Zenith Corporation. Mr Polley is the father of the TV remote control being the inventor of the Flash-Matic.   Yes back in 1955 when they knew how to name things, TV viewers could for the first time switch channels using wireless technology.

According to my limited research the control was Pistol shaped and used a visible light that, once fired against photocells fitted in the corners of the TV screen, could adjust the volume and switch the receiver on and off. Whilst we take this for granted in 2012, it was cutting edge back then and it was many years before the TV remote became common place in Kerswell homes.

The use of visible light was sadly flawed as the photocells would also react to bright sunlight causing the channel to change or the volume to be muted without warning.

It was another Zenith Corporation engineer, Robert Adler who improved the control by using sound waves. His first design was christened the 'Space Command'; I told you they knew how to name things back then! In the 1960s he introduced an ultrasound version that was used until the switch to Infra Red Technology in the 1980s.

Sadly neither of these brilliant men are with us today. Eugene Polley died in May this year aged 96. Robert Adler was 93 when he passed away in 2007. Apparently Adler considered his invention to be one of his lesser inventions. Polley was more enthusiastic and is reputed to have said that the TV remote was the greatest thing since the wheel and that he and Adler "did something for humanity." They shared an Emmy award for their efforts.

So as the dark evenings draw in, and if the clouds are concealing the night sky, and you have turned the sitting room upside down in the hunt for the remote, remember that it was not that long ago when you would have had to get up from the sofa to switch channels and look at it in a new 'infra red' light.

October 2012

Didn't we have a lovely time the day we went to Sherborne!

My regular reader will recall that just outside this Dorset town in a quiet country lane sits the oldest 'in service' pillar box in the country. So on one sunny Saturday in September Sue and I set off, roof down, to Sherborne. Try saying that after a glass or two of Vino Collapso.

One of my sources suggests that this ancient box was only the third cast in the country and speculates why Anthony Trollope chose such a remote spot for the early introduction of postal services. In truth it is thought that this box was relocated from a more prominent site.

Before you ask, yes that Anthony Trollope, responsible for the Barchester and Palliser Novels. Before he was able to rely on his royalties, he made his living as a Post Office surveyor organising early rural postal services in mainland Britain. He is accredited with the introduction of pillar boxes.

As we arrived, so did the postman. We were treated to a full guided tour of the box as the letters were collected and he posed for photos. Perhaps you had to be there to appreciate the moment. Interestingly (yes it is!) the box is only around 3 feet tall and slightly neglected having suffered a little subsidence. It seems that the Post Office maintenance crew have been busy elsewhere with their gold paint and so it was that postie asked if we had seen the gold box in Sherborne.

We sped off into the town centre in search of Gold. Outside the Post Office, shimmering in the sunlight, in honour of Peter Wilson's Olympic Gold Medal, sits the double aperture gold pillar box. Yes double - do keep up - he won the double trap shooting medal! The gold boxes will remain for six months.

If that is not enough, Sherborne is also home to a particularly rare Ludlow Wall Box and an anonymous Handyside Box so another trip is in the offing. We may offer excursions for the very keen. Please form an orderly queue.

Being a sunny day we did not catch site of Undulatus Asperatus. Roughly translated means roughened or agitated waves and has been proposed as a new classification of cloud formation by the Cloud Appreciation Society (it really exists). The race is on as the UN are considering publishing a new edition of the International Cloud Atlas. It is quite extraordinary what the UN do! If included it will be the first new recognised formation for 60 years. Lets hope their judgment isn't clouded!

November 2012

Windsocks

Have you ever considered: What is a Windsock? What is the purpose of a Windsock? How do Windsocks work? Where would you buy a Windsock? What is the origin of Windsocks? How do you read a Windsock?

No? Go on hasn't everyone? Either way you can rest easy as I have done a little (and I mean a little) research.

A windsock is a 'conical textile tube' which indicates wind speed and direction. It is not an air sock which delivers conditioned air. Nor is it a winsock which is an abbreviation for Windows Sockets API (WSA), a technical specification that defines how Windows network software should access network services. Wake up, it's not that boring!

Now, you might think that the workings of a windsock were simple. Not so, there are aerodynamics involved and the conical shape is essential to its operation creating compression and lift. For your windsock to work you will also need a sock hoop which holds the cone open and of course a swivel to allow it to rotate to catch the wind.

Now curtail your excitement as there are a couple of things to consider before you rush out and buy a windsock!

There are plenty of places where you can buy a windsock including Snettisham, Norfolk. Here kite and windsock shop owner Neil Grant has been told by his local council to remove the fluttering socks as they are a distraction to motorists. So windsock positioning is important.

Additionally what are you going to use your windsock for? A landing guide for Santa perhaps? Early warning of a chemical explosion - steady with the sprouts! Simple decoration or for celebration? Originally the Japanese used to fly a windsock to announce the birth of a baby boy. Today they fly Koinobori or carp shaped windsocks to celebrate the national holiday of Tango no Sekku or Children's Day on May 5. The Romans also used windsocks as military banners - no I wasn't there.

Of course if you happen to own an airport, and who doesn't, you will need a windsock. There are a number of specialist providers on the internet. In the UK windsocks must comply with CAA CAP 168, ICAO Annex 14. This requires that at least one wind sleeve should be provided at an aerodrome and should measure 12ft long with a 3ft opening tapering to 1ft. It should be coloured to give maximum contrast to its surroundings.

In the US the Federal Aviation Authority require that a windsock will be fully extended in a 15 knot wind (17 mph). At 3 knots (3.5 mph) it should swivel to catch the wind.

I feel a visit to Dunkeswell and the gliding club coming on! Lucky Sue.

Before wishing you a Happy Christmas there is a final piece of 2012 post box news - bet you thought I wasn't going to mention them - the post office have decided that the gold boxes have become 'cherished local landmarks' and are to stay gold. Good enough to send any Frankincense and Myrrh you happen to have lying about.

I look forward to boring you further next year.

December 2012

A gentle wind fills the windsock at Dunkeswell. Lucky Sue missed this exciting moment,

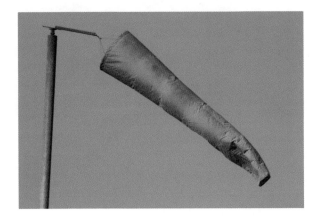

When Clyde met Sharon

They are everywhere. On tins of soup, M&S knicker labels and deliveries. They track parcels and update stock levels in supermarkets. They allow us to check out our own groceries - how were we conned into saving Tesco's staff wages? Note feelings of outrage although the self checkout is the only place I am still asked if I am over 18 so it can't be all bad! You might even find one on a DFS sofa delivery - just spotted that they have a sale, must rush!

Yes, I am talking about Bar Codes. Those odd strips of thin and thick black lines that identify whatever they are attached to. Of course there are other Bar Codes; rules of the pub or perhaps the pin number for the door! Alternatively the term Bar Code might be interpreted as rules for barristers. Can you speak for a minute on Bar Codes without hesitation, repetition or deviation?

One of the most exciting things about Bar Codes is that at the time of their patent on 7 October 1952 they were far ahead of their time. The equipment to scan them wasn't available until some years later. In case you don't have a note it is US Patent No. 2,612,994.

There is considerable information about the development of Bar Codes on the web and I know you will already be looking it up. The most early use was for the identification of railway trucks across the US. Different patterns were considered including bullseye, starburst and linear designs. In 1970 the U.S. Supermarket Ad Hoc Committee on a Uniform Grocery Product Code was established to set out the parameters for its development and use. The 11 digit identification code upon which the Bar Code relies was born (buzz in for repetition of identification!).

Bar Wars followed as RCA and IBM competed for their versions to be adopted. There was a new hope when the first trial in a supermarket commenced in July 1972 at the Kroger Supermarket in Cincinnati using the RCA bullseye system. However this system failed to hit the spot as the ink tended to smear and the codes became unreadable. The IBM empire struck back with the linear code that was finally adopted. Any smears simply extended the length of the bar.

Now brace yourself because here is the best bit. The first commercial use of the Unified Product Code was on 26 June 1974 at Marsh's Supermarket in Troy, Ohio. Clyde Dawson bought a pack of Wrigley's Juicy Fruit gum. It was scanned by Sharon Buchanan at 8:01 am. The pack of gum and the receipt are now apparently held by the Smithsonian Institution. Now there's somewhere to add to my list of places to visit. Lucky Sue.

February 2013

Global Tracking

It is often said that you can wait for a bus for ages and then two come along at once. Whilst even one is unlikely in Kerswell it seems that celestial bodies are more common.

This year the warm coat and the home telescope are on stand by as we await the arrival of two - yes two - Comets. Yes it is quite exciting and I am told that Comet's recent financial difficulties and subsequent administration will have no impact on these meteoric events. The first, Pann-Starrs, should appear sometime in March within a mere 102 million miles of Kerswell. If you miss it Comet Ison promises to be more spectacular in the Autumn just 40 million miles overhead so make sure your windsock is not flying too high.

These events will take me away from what are proving to be the most compelling websites ever. I feel it is my duty to share them with you. The first is http://www.marinetraffic.com/ais/. My other reader obviously thought I had too much time on my hands and was kind enough to draw my attention to it. The site allows you to track the movement of commercial shipping and access photographs and statistics about individual boats.

As I write I can see the Gaschem Bremen is anchored in the Panama Canal under a Liberian Flag. It is an LPG Tanker some 173 metres in length on its way to Lazaro Cardenas wherever that is. Meanwhile Roman Abramovich's 163 metre yacht the Eclipse is moored in Bermuda. Where else? Apparently it is available for charter; Gin & Tonic anyone or perhaps a run across to France for some Vino Collapso? The winter nights are just sailing by here.

If a trip over the briny doesn't float your boat then how about a flight of fancy from your front room. Take a look at www.flightradar24.com. Check which flights are passing over Kerswell. Flight BY417 is about to pass over on its way to Manchester from Boa Vista - its Cape Verde off the coast of Gambia! I knew that, perhaps I'll sail there when I charter the Eclipse! Track down Boeing Dreamliners if they are flying and the massive Airbus A380 and then link to planespotters.net for photos and statistics about the aircraft you are watching. If that is not enough excitement you can link to Google Earth to get the Cockpit view. Its flying without the jet lag! Check your windsock again before coming into land! Back on the ground it's like a virtual game of top trumps - I have a Boeing 767 at 460 knots.

Perhaps I need to get out more! Pothole Spotting may be an option - see www.potholes.co.uk

March 2013

Pothole Spotting - extra points for this shapely example.

An Exciting Day in Kerswell

Since my exciting report of Kerswell's Edward VII letterbox, I have entertained / interested / bored (delete as appropriate) you and my other reader with all manner of useful and stimulating information. Clouds, Pylons, Windsocks and Roundabouts have all come under the Sandy Way scrutiny. Last month it was a few websites for you to try; sadly two addresses were lost in flight to the printers - www.flightradar24.com and planespotters.net. I hope you weren't too distraught. Perhaps they were censored as a breach of security.

This has all been at the expense of giving deserved attention to our own village amenities and it was always just a matter of time before my head turned to the study of the telephone box. OK, it doesn't actually have a telephone in it, Presumably a result of the growing use of the mobile phone. All very well but when I went to the box to make my telephone call I had no signal.

The K series of red telephone boxes remain a familiar site across Britain and its dependent territories. The original K2 design by Sir Giles Gilbert Scott was developed in successive models culminating in the K6 that we have in Kerswell. My favourite has to be the K4 designed in 1927. Only 50 were ever made and combined a telephone box, post box and stamp vending machine - how great is that? Nicknamed the vermillion giant, I believe there may be one on the East Somerset Railway. I feel a trip in the offing - lucky Sue.

Now here is something to look for. Prior to 1955 all telephone boxes, as in Kerswell, carried the Tudor Crown upon their fascias. This was the symbol of government at the time. It was replaced following Queen Elizabeth's ascension to the throne by the more familiar St. Edward's Crown used at the coronation.

1968 saw the introduction of the K8. Bigger windows, brighter red and more prone to damage and vandalism. According to The Guardian, 11,000 were installed but only 12 have survived in use - 4 of which are in Swindon. Designed by Bruce Martin - you know - that Bruce Martin, architect born 20 December 1917 and, well that's all I have so far! The K9 was, you will recall, a robot dog.

It is now over 20 years since Neil Papworth sent the first text message. Mobile phones have moved on since you needed a small van to carry the battery. When the telephone network was privatised phone boxes became less distinctive and certainly less iconic. We should be proud to have our very own K6, even without a phone. What an exciting day it must have been when it was installed; does anyone remember it? And the K? Kiosk of course!

April 2013

K6 Telephone Kiosk, Kerswell.

Vol. 2 coming soon to a website near you!

Printed in Great Britain
by Amazon.co.uk, Ltd.,
Marston Gate.

THE INCREDIBLE HULK

INSIDE....

SECRET MISSION...

General Ross has sent 10 military spy bugs in search of Bruce Banner. Can you spot them all hidden throughout these pages?

£6.99

CW00449065

ORIGINS......

BEFORE THE HULK...

Bruce Banner was the most gifted physicist of his generation. A genius in the field of particle physics, it wasn't long before his reputation attracted the attention of Bio-Tech, a military enhancement program connected to his college science faculty...

HULK FACTS: The madder Hulk gets, the bigger and stronger he gets!

THE BEGINNING...

Along with fellow scientist and girlfriend, Betty Ross, Bruce was recruited by Betty's father, General "Thunderbolt" Ross to work on a cutting-edge cellular enhancement program. Using low levels of gamma radiation, the treatment was intended to boost the strength and healing power of special forces soldiers, giving them the edge in battle. And one day, after months of lab work, Bruce made a breakthrough...

HULK FACTS: Bruce has refused to contact Betty until he finds a cure!

A TERRIBLE ACCIDENT...

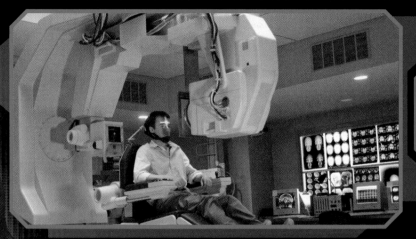

Bruce was so convinced by his discovery that he decided to test the serum on himself. With the assistance of his team, which included Betty, Bruce injected the serum into his bloodstream, strapped himself into the gamma chair and began to absorb the radiation. But something went terribly wrong and the machine exploded – leaving Betty critically injured in a coma. And as for Bruce, a far worse fate awaited...

MUTATION...

The massive amount of gamma radiation Bruce absorbed should have killed him. But due to the protection of the serum in his blood, he woke up without a scratch. The damage, he'd soon find out, went much deeper, to the very core of his being – his DNA! And so the Hulk was born...

DNA MUTATION SCAN

MOOD GENE

When Banner discovered what he'd become, his life, as he knew it, was over. And he blamed himself. Not just for his own condition, but for Betty's injuries. All he wanted to do was disappear. But General Ross had other ideas...

HULK FACTS:
Bruce started learning Aikido in Brazil to help keep his anger under control!

HUNTED...

Having seen the terrifying power of the Hulk in action, Ross had only one aim – to capture the monster and use it as a super-weapon. Hunted to the ends of the earth, Bruce ended up hiding in the slums of Brazil, where for the past five years he's been working obsessively towards his life's only goal – a cure...

Believing it might act as a Hulk 'inhibitor', Bruce has been extracting a chemical called Tri-Methodine from rare exotic flowers.

BANNER'S CASE FILES...

In order to try to understand the Hulk, Banner's recorded a case-file on every Hulk 'episode' right from the start. Now, for the first time ever, he's allowing YOU to read them...

#34R – DUPED

LOCATION: Downtown Manhattan
PARTIES INVOLVED: Multiple Man, Rick Jones
COST IN DAMAGE: £36,345,546
CASE NOTES: Searching for a cure to finally rid myself of the Hulk, I was trying to track down an old physicist friend of mine. The plan was to use his gamma radiation equipment in his secret lab to reverse my mutation process. All I needed to do was find the lab...

RICK JONES

Rick's my most trusted friend and has been helping me out since this whole nightmare began. I guess that goes for his side-kick, Monkey, too, though sometimes he's more trouble than he's worth!

THE MULTIPLE MAN

Jamie Madrox, aka the Multiple Man, is a human mutant with the ability to create duplicates, or 'dupes' of himself. He's a good guy, though some of his dupes can be a little less friendly.

YOUR MISSION

Pay attention during the action as Banner will need your help to fill a few gaps in his case-files. Ok, go to the next page and begin»»»

14

MISSIONS...
HUNTED!

General Ross and half the U.S. Army are chasing after Hulk!
Can you help him get away before New York city becomes a
war-zone? Finish all tasks to complete the mission!

 INTERCEPTED! We've picked up a scrambled radio message from
Ross to his troops. Can you unscramble it to find out his plan?

ROSS! SET UP   THE DOUBLE!   PARK! ON

IN CENTRAL   AN AMBUSH   THIS IS GENERAL

 ESCAPE ROUTE! Nice work. OK, Ross is planning an ambush in Central Park. Guide
Hulk through the city to Times Square by avoiding the helicopters AND Central Park!

START

CENTRAL PARK

TIMES SQUARE

3.

A TRAP! Uh oh, the radio message from Ross was a trick! The real ambush is in Times Square and Hulk's walked right into it! Help Hulk fight by spotting 10 dangers!

4.

HACKED OFF! OK, Hulk escaped Times Square and is on the run again. Help him shake Ross off for good by hacking into the army's radar computer and shutting it down!

INSTRUCTIONS:

1. To find the shut-down password, cross out all the words as you find them.

2. Write the left-over letters into the datapad.

B	H	U	L	K	T
A	R	M	Y	G	A
N	U	K	E	E	N
N	N	N	E	R	K
E	B	R	U	C	E
R	O	S	S	A	L

HULK

NUKE   **BRUCE**

RUN   ARMY   TANK

ROSS   BANNER

19

21

22

DE-BRIEFING....

OK, there are a few details Banner's still hazy on. Can you help? Tick the correct answer to each question to update his case-files.

1. Where did the action take place?

a) London ☐   b) Paris ☐   c) Manhattan ☐

2. Who is this?

a) Rick Jones ☐

b) Jamie Madrox ☐

c) Jimmy Badsox ☐

 **A**

 **B**

 **C**

3. Look at the three computer screens to the left. Which one were they REALLY looking at?

4. What was Hulk REALLY saying?

A Hulk crush puny humans!

B Arrrgh, no pepperoni!

C It okay, Hulk save you!

5. Can you spot four things we've changed in the scene below?

TURN TO PAGE 62 TO CHECK YOUR ANSWERS!

ABOMINATION!

There are many that want to destroy the Hulk. But of all his enemies, he has perhaps only one true nemesis. They call it the Abomination...

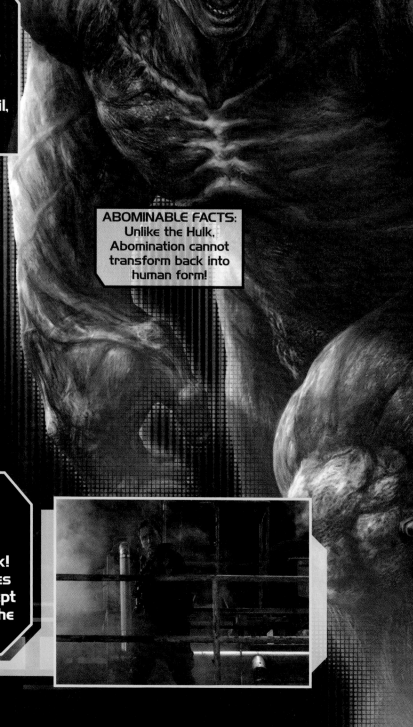

EMIL BLONSKY...

One of the U.S. Army's most skilled special forces soldiers, Emil Blonsky lives for combat. As the leader of an ultra-secret black ops unit, Blonsky's the man they turn to when a job needs to get done quickly, and quietly. So when General Ross tracks Banner down to the backstreet slums of Brazil, Blonsky gets his orders - to capture Banner alive and bring him in...

ABOMINABLE FACTS: Unlike the Hulk, Abomination cannot transform back into human form!

FIRST CONTACT...

But when Blonsky and his team storm Banner's apartment, the doc makes a run for it. The operation turns messy, and when the pressure gets too much for Banner, he transforms into the Hulk! The sight of the ferocious beast freezes everyone in their tracks. Everyone except Blonsky, who is transfixed, in awe of the monster's sheer rage and power...

KNOWLEDGE IS POWER...

After the mission, Blonsky forces a full explanation out of Ross. When he hears about the Super Soldier Serum, he convinces the General to be allowed a small dose. His plan - to gain enough power to take on the Hulk himself!

MUTATION...

ABOMINABLE FACTS: It's believed that Blonsky, like Bruce Banner, belongs to a small minority of humans born with a genetic factor that responds to gamma exposure by mutation instead of death.

At first the injection is a complete success, giving Blonsky unnaturally high speed, strength and healing ability. But then something goes horribly wrong, and Blonsky mutates even more horrifically than Banner himself! An 11 foot 'abomination' of scales and muscle, Blonsky finds himself unable to transform back into his human form. And now there's only one thing on his mind - destroying his ultimate enemy, the Hulk!

HULK VS ABOMINATION

While being as strong as Hulk in a calm state, the Abomination's strength does not increase with his anger as the Hulk's does. It is also thought that his healing power is weaker than the Hulk's, taking his tissue cells more time to reproduce after damage. But if Hulk has the edge physically, Abomination makes up for it in pure rage, hate and determination! One thing's for sure, when these two meet, it's gonna get messy!

PROFILES....

GENERAL THADDEUS ROSS

AKA: General "Thunderbolt" Ross
Status: Enemy
Bio: Head of the ultra-secret Super Soldier program that accidentally caused Banner's mutation, Ross believes the Hulk is U.S. Army property, and plans to harness his power as a weapon. He's also father to Banner's ex-girlfriend, Betty Ross, and is determined to keep her safe by keeping them apart. Ross won't rest until Banner - and the Hulk - are under his control.

Despite having the entire might of the U.S. Army behind him, Ross hasn't yet found a way of trapping the Incredible Hulk.

GENERAL GRELLER

Status: Enemy
Bio: An old friend of Ross' from the Vietnam war, General Greller is one of the few people the hard-headed Ross will listen to.

DR ELIZABETH ROSS

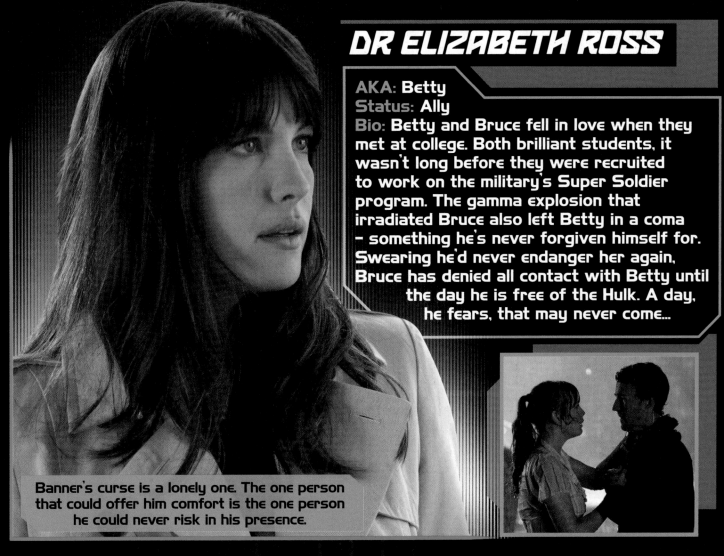

AKA: Betty
Status: Ally
Bio: Betty and Bruce fell in love when they met at college. Both brilliant students, it wasn't long before they were recruited to work on the military's Super Soldier program. The gamma explosion that irradiated Bruce also left Betty in a coma – something he's never forgiven himself for. Swearing he'd never endanger her again, Bruce has denied all contact with Betty until the day he is free of the Hulk. A day, he fears, that may never come...

Banner's curse is a lonely one. The one person that could offer him comfort is the one person he could never risk in his presence.

SAMUEL STERNS

AKA: Mr Blue
Status: Ally
Bio: A physics professor in the same field as Banner, Sterns may be Banner's only hope of finding a cure. Under the alias of Mr Green and Mr Blue, Bruce and Sterns began work on a Hulk 'inhibitor' when Bruce was in hiding in Brazil.

DR LEONARD SAMSON

Status: Ally
Bio: Samson is Betty Ross' new boyfriend. A good man and a gifted psychiatrist, Samson knows deep down that Betty has never really stopped thinking about Bruce since his disappearance five years ago.

BANNER'S CASE FILES

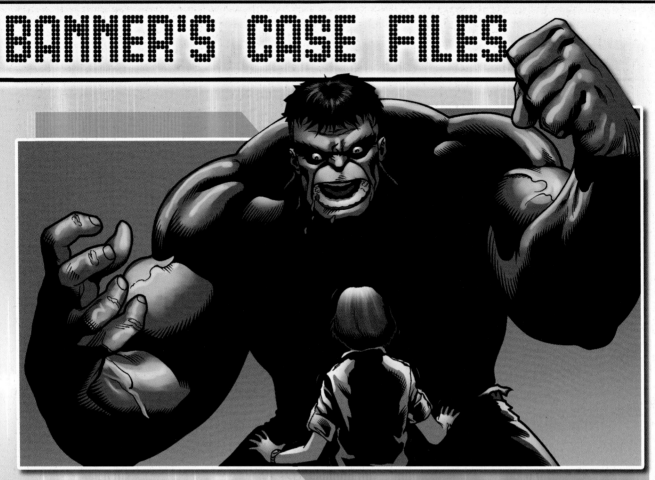

#67G – DESERTED

Location: New Mexico Desert
Parties involved: Dr Leonard Samson, Betty Ross, Rick Jones
Cost in damage: E2,353,061
Case notes: A million miles from anywhere in the middle of the New Mexico Desert, the last person I expected to see was Betty. But when she and travel companion, Dr Samson, explained they'd developed a cure for my condition, it all seemed just a little too good to be true...

DR LEONARD SAMSON

One of the world's most brilliant psychiatrists, Samson has always been fascinated by my alter-ego, the Hulk. Despite appearances, he's really just an ordinary science nerd like me. The Greek God look is a recent thing - a side effect of gamma radiation experiments of his own, conducted to help find my cure.

YOUR MISSION

Keep your eyes peeled during the action because Banner will need your help again to update his case-files. Ok, go to the next page and begin»»»

It's really her, Bruce.

L...Leonard?!

Uh...Rick Jones, meet Dr. Leonard Samson. One of the world's most brilliant psychiatrists.

I'm no Bruce Banner--but I'm not entirely adrift in the nuclear physics department either.

Doc Samson...? Yeah...Bruce's mentioned you... briefly.

Bruce... Leonard and I have been working together to find a cure for your... condition.

Unless Leonard's been pumping iron and listening to alt. rock since I last saw him, I'm guessing he's already tested gamma radiation on himself.

What gave me away?

I also set up gamma sensors in places where I theorized your subconscious mind might lead Hulk.

Hacked my phone to pick up the signal as soon as you went near one. Cool, eh?

41

"Betty and I have designed a combination of psychotherapy and low-dosage radiation treatments to suppress the triggers that cause your transformation."

General Ross gave Betty carte blanche to continue your work after the... accident.

First time I was ever glad to be a military brat...

Betty's father has no clue that we've been using this facility to find a cure.

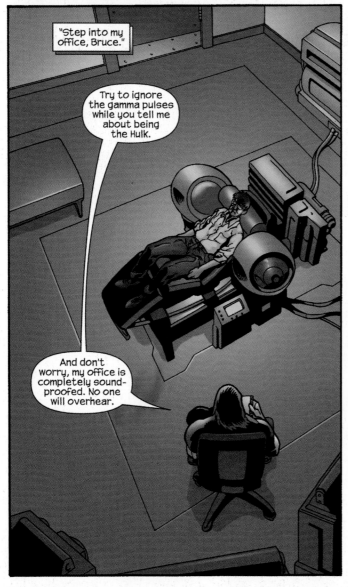

"Step into my office, Bruce."

Try to ignore the gamma pulses while you tell me about being the Hulk.

And don't worry, my office is completely sound-proofed. No one will overhear.

Okay... ummm...think about your own gamma-boosted strength.

You could punch a man through a brick wall, right?

This isn't about me, Bruce.

Now imagine being constantly afraid you'll lose control of those fists...getting angry and waking up to find out you've leveled a small town.

43

44

Incredible, Leonard!

A safe place is the key to psychotherapy, Bruce.

If you don't keep your emotions bottled up, you'll be less...explosive... under stress.

You'll need several more radiation treatments and ongoing therapy to make it permanent.

We just need to take a break while your body absorbs the radiation.

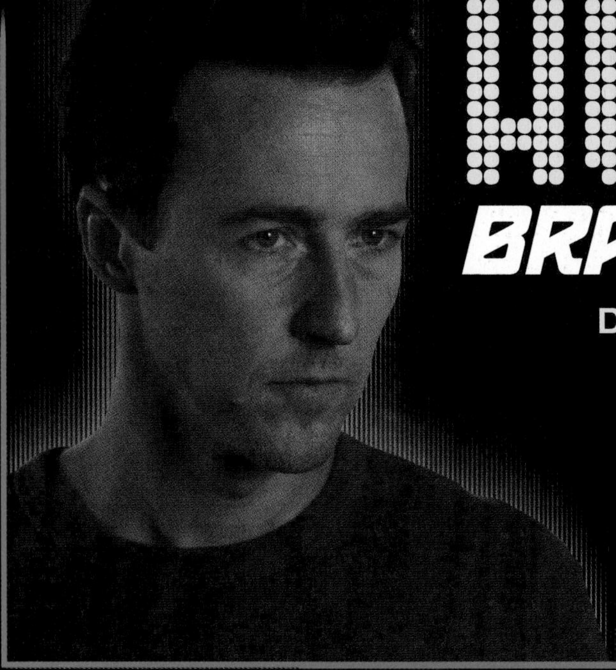

HULK TEST
BRAINS OVER BRAUN

Dr Bruce Banner's always looking for smart allies to help him search for his cure. He's devised this test to see whether you make the grade!

1. What was Banner trying to extract his cure from?

A. Frogs ☐   B. Flowers ☐   C. Fruit ☐

2. What country was Banner hiding in?

A. Brazil ☐
B. Spain ☐
C. Mexico ☐

3. Look closely at this picture. Can you spot 4 things that should not be there?

- ☐
- ☐
- ☐
- ☐

4. Look at this sliced up photo. Tick the piece that does not belong.

5. Can you spot 6 differences between these two scenes?

6. Which martial art has Banner studied to control his anger?

A. Aikido

B. Kick Boxing

C. Ju-Jitsu

9. Who's been snapped by each spy camera?

7. What does Ross give to Blonsky to make him tougher?

A. Tri-methodine

B. Super Soldier Serum

C. Uranium Milkshake

8. What's General Ross' nickname?

A. Smartbomb

B. Cruise-missile

C. Thunderbolt

   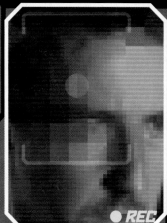

● REC   ● REC   ● REC   ● REC

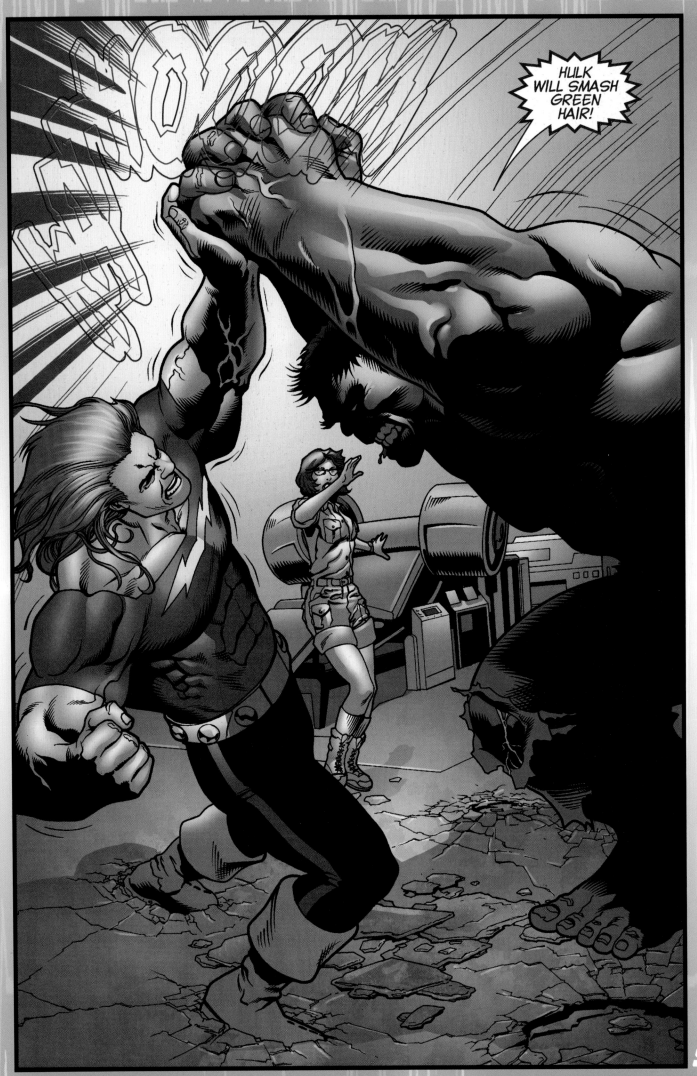

DE-BRIEFING...

Just like before, Banner needs your help to fill in some gaps in his case-file records. Tick the correct answer in each section.

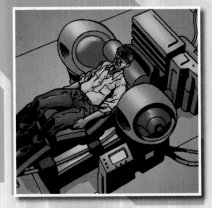

1. What was Samson's new treatment?

a) A reverse gamma ray

b) Behaviour therapy combined with gamma rays

c) Gamme rays combined with massage

2. Gamma rays have corrupted this surveillance image. Can you find four things that should NOT be there?

3. Look at the image below. Who was this shadowy figure behind Banner?

a) Rick Jones

b) Dr Samson

c) Betty Ross

4. This security photo was shredded during the action. Can you find the only piece that doesn't belong?

5. Look at the action shot below. What happened next?

a) Banner punched Samson

b) Banner cried

c) Banner turned into Hulk

6. Can you put these events into the right order?

TURN TO PAGE 62 TO CHECK YOUR ANSWERS!

ANSWERS....

DE-BRIEFING

1=C, 2=A, 3=C,
4. "IT OKAY, HULK SAVE YOU!",

HUNTED

1. "THIS IS GENERAL ROSS! SET UP AN AMBUSH IN CENTRAL PARK! ON THE DOUBLE!"

2.

START
FINISH

3.
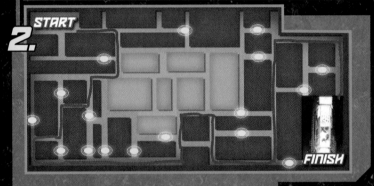

4. Shutdown password is GENERAL.

5.

DE-BRIEFING 2

1=A, 3=C, 4=E, 5=C.

2.

5.

5. 2. 1. 3. 4.

HULK TEST

1=B, 2=A,

3.

4.

5.

6=A, 7=B, 8=C. 9. Ross, Betty, Blonsky and Banner were snapped by the spy cam.

SECRET MISSION

The spy bugs were hidden on pages 4, 6, 18, 19, 31, 33, 34, 35, 46, 47.